HOW BIG IS A
BRACHIOSAURUS?

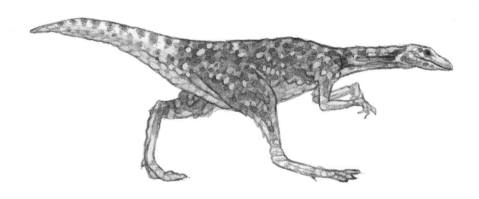

Hippo Books
Scholastic Publications Ltd
London

HOW BIG IS A

Scholastic Publications Ltd., 10 Earlham Street, London WC2H 9RX, UK.
Scholastic Inc., 730 Broadway, New York, NY 10003, USA. Scholastic Tab
Publicatons Ltd., 123 Newkirk Road, Richmond Hill, Ontario L4C 3G5,
Canada. Ashton Scholastic Pty. Ltd., P O Box 579, Gosford, New South
Wales, Australia. Ashton Scholastic Ltd., 165 Marua Road, Panmure,
Auckland 6, New Zealand. First published in the USA and Canada by the
Putnam Publishing Group, 1986. Published in the UK by Scholastic Publica-
tions Ltd., 1988. Text Copyright © Platt & Munk, 1986. Illustrations

BRACHIOSAURUS?

Fascinating Facts About Dinosaurs

By Susan Carroll
Illustrated by Frederic Marvin

PSITTACOSAURUS

Has anyone ever seen a dinosaur that was alive?

No. Dinosaurs died out, or became extinct, about 65 million years ago, many millions of years before human beings appeared on the earth.

What does "dinosaur" mean?

The word is from the Greek and means "terrible lizard". A dinosaur is any one of a large group of animals classified as reptiles that lived on the earth long ago — over a period of about 140 million years.

Do we know about dinosaurs just from the bones that have been dug up?

No. We know about them from fossils of all kinds. A fossil is any trace of a living thing that has been preserved in rock. We get information about dinosaurs from fossilized bones, teeth, eggs, skin, stomach contents, footprints, and other fossil clues.

Which dinosaur was the longest?

The longest, measuring from head to tail, was a huge, four-legged, plant-eating creature named Diplodocus (dih-PLOD-uh-kus). The animal grew as long as 27m, or the length of three buses. However, it was also slender and only weighed about 12 tonnes.

Which dinosaur was the heaviest?

The one that weighed the most was a gigantic but gentle plant-eater named Brachiosaurus (BRAK-ee-uh-sawr-us).
This animal could weigh 70 or 80 tonnes, as much as ten or twelve African elephants. Only one museum in the world, in East Berlin, has mounted a whole skeleton. The skeleton stands taller than a four-storey building.

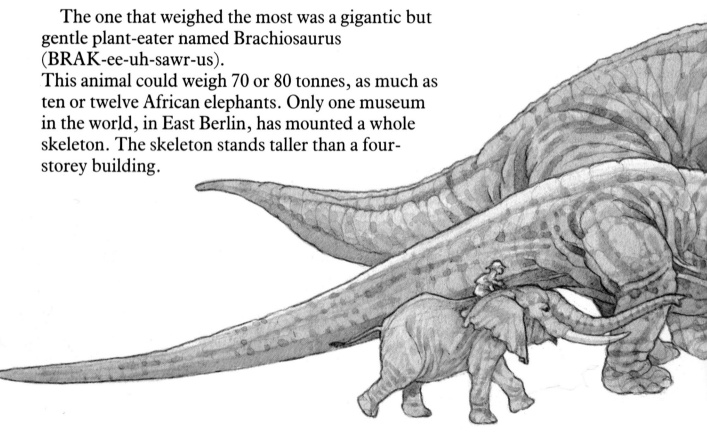

BRACHIOSAURUS

DIPLODOCUS

Were there any small dinosaurs?

Yes. Some were smaller than a human being.

A fast little meat-eater named Saltopus (SALT-o-pus) only weighed one kilogram, less than a cat.

SALTOPUS

The tiny Compsognathus (komp-sog-NAY-thus), which means "pretty jaw", was about the size of a chicken. It was very bird-like and may even have had feathers.

COMPSOGNATHUS

One of the best-known small dinosaurs was the lightly-built, two-metre long Ornitholestes (or-nith-o-LESS-teez). Its name means "bird robber" because it is supposed to have caught flying reptiles.

ORNITHOLESTES

The smallest dinosaur skeleton discovered so far is a very young hatchling Psittacosaurus (sit-uh-ko-SAWR-us), or "parrot lizard". This baby dinosaur was the size of a small bird.

PSITTACOSAURUS

What did dinosaurs like to eat?

Most were plant-eaters, or herbivores. Some were meat-eaters, or carnivores. A few ate both plants and meat.

How much did the big plant-eating dinosaurs eat?

Scientists aren't sure, but the biggest plant-eaters, such as Apatosaurus (ah-PAT-uh-sawr-us), better known as Brontosaurus, must have eaten all day long. However, they did not have to stop and chew their food. These dinosaurs swallowed leaves and small branches whole. The food was ground up in their stomachs by stones that they swallowed.

Scientists used to think all dinosaurs were cold-blooded, in which case Apatosaurus would have eaten about 130kg of plant food each day. If the giant was warm-blooded, which might have been the case, it would have had to eat as much as 900kg a day.

APATOSAURUS

TYRANNOSAURUS

PARASAUROLOPHUS

How much did meat-eating dinosaurs eat?

One of the biggest, fiercest meat-eating dinosaurs was Tyrannosaurus rex (tye-RAN-uh-sawr-us rex), or "king tyrant lizard". For food, it attacked plant-eating dinosaurs. It is thought that this eight-tonne animal could eat as much as 200kg of meat at one time. Afterwards it probably would not eat again for several days.

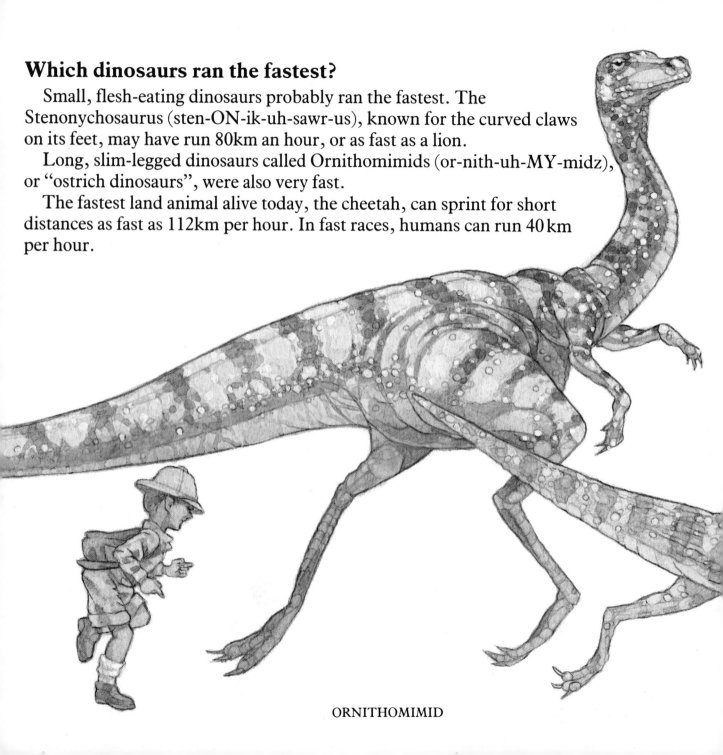

Which dinosaurs ran the fastest?

Small, flesh-eating dinosaurs probably ran the fastest. The Stenonychosaurus (sten-ON-ik-uh-sawr-us), known for the curved claws on its feet, may have run 80km an hour, or as fast as a lion.

Long, slim-legged dinosaurs called Ornithomimids (or-nith-uh-MY-midz), or "ostrich dinosaurs", were also very fast.

The fastest land animal alive today, the cheetah, can sprint for short distances as fast as 112km per hour. In fast races, humans can run 40km per hour.

ORNITHOMIMID

Could dinosaurs climb trees?

Probably not.
Their stiff ankle joints
would have made
it difficult.

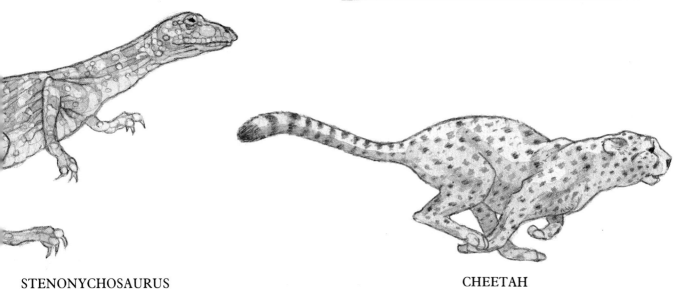

STENONYCHOSAURUS

CHEETAH

Did some dinosaurs move slowly?

Yes. Dinosaurs with thick, short legs were probably very slow. The tank-like Ankylosaurus (ang-KILE-uh-sawr-us), or "armoured lizard", which grew as long as 7m, probably moved along at less than 8km per hour.

The huge sauropods, such as Apatosaurus and Brachiosaurus, lumbered forward slowly as well.

There are far slower land animals on the earth today. Some turtles move at only 400m per hour.

How do scientists know if dinosaurs were fast or slow?

They can figure it out by measuring fossilized dinosaur tracks. The faster an animal runs, the longer its strides.

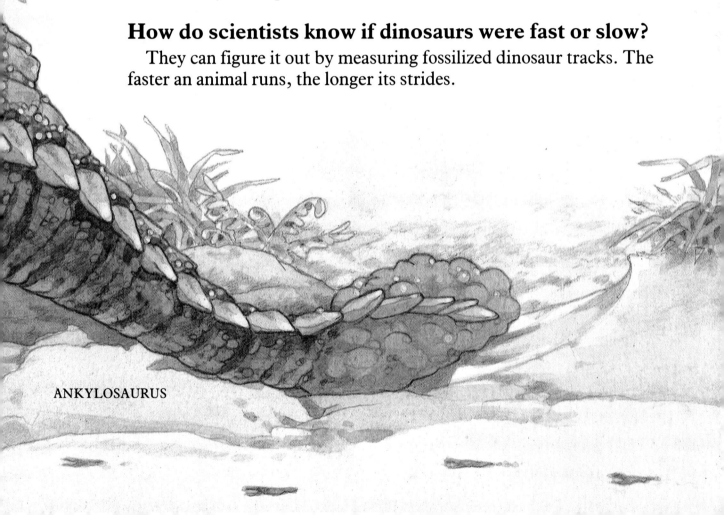

ANKYLOSAURUS

Did dinosaurs have sharp teeth?

The meat-eaters did. They needed sharp, pointed teeth, often notched like a saw, to catch and eat their prey.

The powerful Tyrannosaurus had as many as 60 knife-like teeth, some of which were 15cm long.

TYRANNOSAURUS

Did plant-eating dinosaurs have teeth?

Yes, but they were smaller and less pointed than teeth belonging to a carnivore.

Hadrosaurs (HAD-ruh-sawrz), or "duck-billed lizards", were plant-eaters. Hadrosaurs, including Kritosaurus (KRY-to-saur-us), had several rows of teeth to help grind tough plant fibres. They had no teeth at the front of their mouths, but inside were as many as 2000 teeth in all!

KRITOSAURUS

Which dinosaurs had the longest claws?

All dinosaurs had claws of some kind on their feet and hands, but the meat-eaters tended to have particularly long and sharp ones.

A huge carnivore named Deinocheirus (dye-nuh-KYE-rus), or "terrible hand", did in fact have frightening hands. Each one was 60cm long. Three fingers on each hand were armed with hook-like claws that were as long as 30cm.

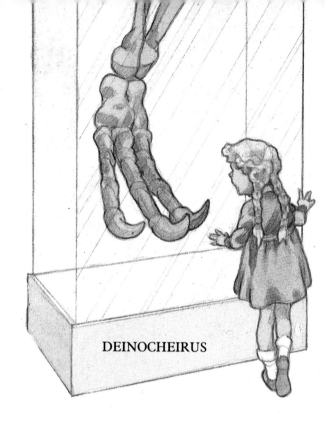

DEINOCHEIRUS

IGUANODON

One of the strangest claws belonged to a two-footed plant-eater named Iguanodon (ig-WAN-oh-don). It had long spikes for thumbs. The spikes grew at right angles to the other four fingers and were probably used as weapons.

TRICERATOPS

Which dinosaurs had horns?

Some plant-eating dinosaurs developed armour to protect themselves from the meat-eaters. Head shields with horns were one form of protection.

The big four-footed Triceratops (try-SAIR-uh-tops), which means "three-horned face", had one short, thick nose-horn and two enormous horns on its brow, growing over 1m long. Triceratops was so well protected by its horns and neck frill that it was one of the last dinosaurs to become extinct.

Which dinosaur had spines on its back?

Spinosaurus (SPY-nur-sawr-us), or the "thorn lizard", was a large meat-eater with a blade on its back somewhat like the fin a sailfish. Covered with skin, the blade had spines in it that were as much as 2m long. The blade may have helped control the animal's body temperature.

SPINOSAURUS

STEGOSAURUS

Which dinosaur had the biggest armour plates?

The Stegosaurus (STEG-uh-sawr-us), or the "plated lizard", was a four-legged plant-eater about the size of an elephant. The large bony plates that ran in two rows down its back grew as big as 60cm wide and 60cm tall. The plates may have helped this animal, too, to control body temperature and to keep meat-eaters away. Stegosaurus also had sharp 30cm spikes at the end of its strong tail.

Which dinosaur left the biggest footprint?

Apatosaurus, one of the huge, elephant-legged sauropods, left footprints over 76cm long. The broad, padded feet of this dinosaur were the size of big bass drums.

Are there many dinosaur footprints left?

Yes. Literally thousands — scattered all over the world, on every continent. In some places, dinosaur parks have been established so that people can visit and see fossilized footprints and tracks.

Why are footprints interesting?

Dinosaur tracks give scientists information they would have trouble learning any other way. Tracks give clues about how and where a dinosaur walked, how fast it moved, whether it herded or hunted with other dinosaurs, whether it knew how to swim, and even how it stalked its prey.

How were baby dinosaurs born?

Dinosaur babies hatched from eggs. Many fossilized eggs have been found in the last 50 years, some with tiny fossil bones inside. Female dinosaurs laid their eggs in nests on the ground.

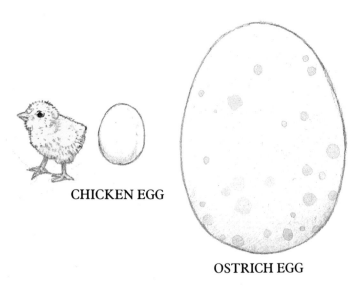

CHICKEN EGG

OSTRICH EGG

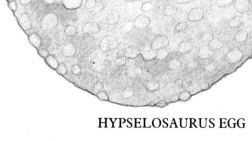

HYPSELOSAURUS EGG

What are the biggest dinosaur eggs ever found?

Roundish eggs twice the size of an ostrich egg have been found in France. They probably belonged to a sauropod called Hypselosaurus (HIP-sih-luh-sawr-us), or "high lizard", referring to its high back. The eggs were found in groups of five, lying in wide, shallow nests dug into the dirt.

MAIASAURA

Did dinosaurs take care of their babies?

Some parents left newly-hatched babies to fend for themselves, but others seem to have cared for their young.

Fifteen baby duckbills known as Maiasaura (mah-ee-ah-SAWR-uh) were found in a nest together not too long ago in the state of Montana. The teeth of the babies already showed a little wear from chewing food. An adult Maiasaura was found nearby. The parent probably brought food to the babies until they were big enough to leave the nest and find food for themselves.

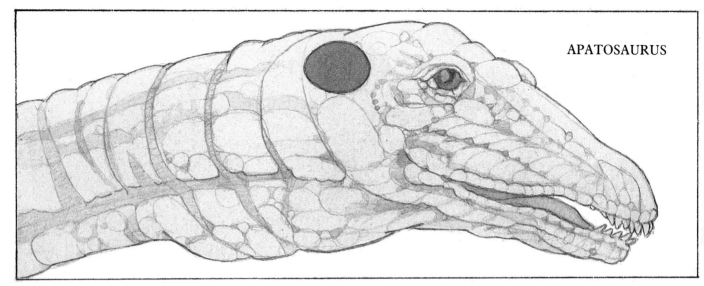

APATOSAURUS

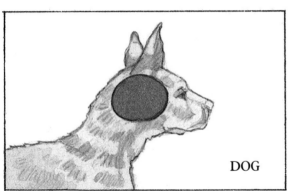

DOG

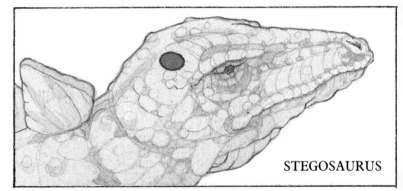

STEGOSAURUS

Were dinosaurs stupid?

People tend to think so because dinosaur heads and brains were often small compared to their huge bodies. The giant sauropods had brains that were only as big as that of a dog. Stegosaurus, the two-tonne, plated dinosaur, had a brain not much bigger than a walnut.

However, new findings suggest that some dinosaurs herded and hunted together, and fed and protected their young. Since these are considered intelligent things to do, the animals were probably cleverer than we had thought.

Did the "thick-headed dinosaurs" get their name because they were stupid?

No. This group of dinosaurs, which included Pachysephalosaurus (pak-ee-SEF-uh-lo-sawr-us), had very thick skulls, as much as 20 times as thick as the bones in a human skull.

PACHYSEPHALOSAURUS

Did dinosaurs have a second brain?

No. But big dinosaurs such as Stegosaurus had large nerve centres in the hip region of their spinal cords. This centre probably controlled the animal's hind legs and huge tail.

STENONYCHOSAURUS

PTERANODON

Did dinosaurs see well?

Yes, probably. And some kinds of dinosaurs undoubtedly saw better than others. The smart, fast predator named Stenonychosaurus would have been able to see especially well. Its eyes were unusually large and spaced far apart so that it would have been able to judge distance very well.

Did dinosaurs have a good sense of smell?

Scientists think so. Nerve roots in the brain and big nasal openings in dinosaur skulls suggest a good sense of smell.

ALLOSAURUS

Are there questions about dinosaurs we can't answer?

Yes. One impossible question is, "What sounds did dinosaurs make?" Scientists think dinosaurs had a good sense of hearing. If so, they must have been able to make sounds, too. But we have no way of knowing if they croaked like frogs or bellowed like elephants.

Another difficult question is, "What colour were dinosaurs?" We know that dinosaurs had tough, leathery skin, often covered with scales, but we can't really know what colour it was. Some dinosaurs may have been as bright as tropical lizards. Many were probably shades of green or brown, colours that would have helped camouflage them from their enemies.

Are people still digging up dinosaur bones today?

Yes. New fossils are being found all the time, in many parts of the world.

In 1972, a few huge bones were found in Colorado that indicated the biggest Brachiosaurid ever found. A single vertebra belonging to "Supersaurus", as it was nicknamed, measured 1.5m long.

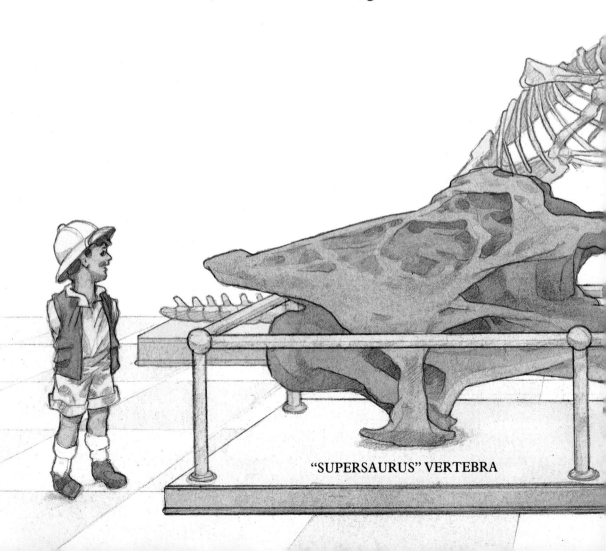

"SUPERSAURUS" VERTEBRA

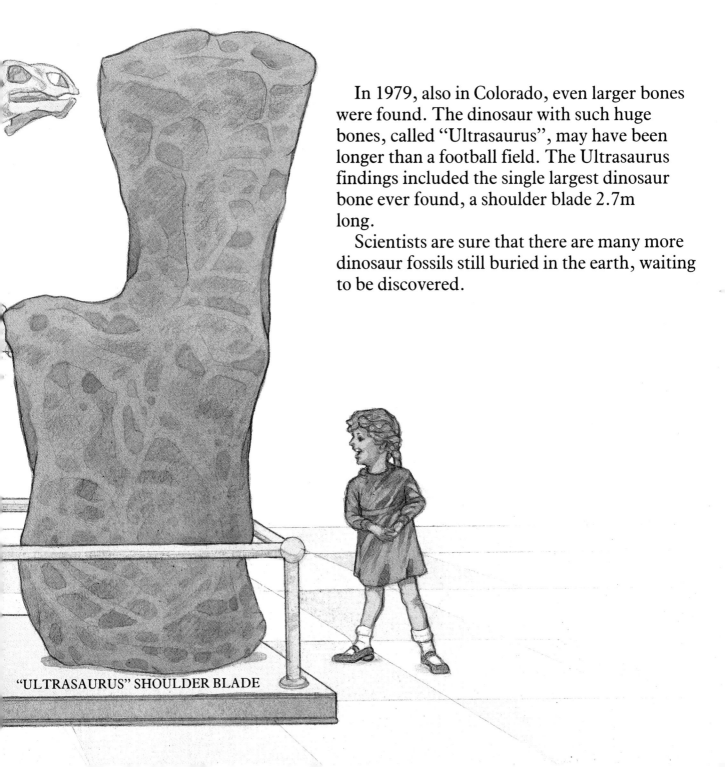

In 1979, also in Colorado, even larger bones were found. The dinosaur with such huge bones, called "Ultrasaurus", may have been longer than a football field. The Ultrasaurus findings included the single largest dinosaur bone ever found, a shoulder blade 2.7m long.

Scientists are sure that there are many more dinosaur fossils still buried in the earth, waiting to be discovered.

"ULTRASAURUS" SHOULDER BLADE

Why did dinosaurs die out?

We don't know for sure. Scientists have a number of theories about what happened 65 million years ago.

Either slowly or quickly, the earth changed in some way. The temperature may have dropped, killing dinosaurs with severe cold. A huge meteor may have hit the earth, heaving dust into the atmosphere and darkening the sky for many months.

Certain animal groups *did* survive whatever changes took place. Some reptiles, insects, early mammals, fish, and birds continued to populate the earth.

CORYPHODON

DIATRYMA